Fish, Shellfish & Vegetables

LOW-FAT KOREAN COOKING

by Noh Chin-hwa
Copyreader: Shirley A. Dorow

HOLLYM INTERNATIONAL CORP.
Elizabeth, New Jersey   Seoul

Copyright © 1985
by Hollym Corporation; Publishers

All rights reserved

First published in 1985
Second printing, 1986
Third printing, 1987
by Hollym International Corp.
18 Donald Place
Elizabeth, New Jersey 07208 U.S.A.

Published simultaneously in Korea
by Hollym Corporation; Publishers
14-5 Kwanchol-dong, Chongno-gu
Seoul, Korea Phone: 735-7554

ISBN: 0-930878-47-7
Library of Congress Catalog Card Number: 85-80451

Printed in Korea

CONTENTS

Author: Noh Chin-hwa

Copyreader: Shirley A. Dorow

About the Author

The author, Noh Chin-hwa, graduated from Seoul National University with a degree in Home Economics. Since her marriage she has put her natural talent in cooking as well as in flower arranging and painting to good use.

Applying her creative power to cooking she has contributed articles and pictures to women's magazines, and she used to give lectures at Home Economics' College and Women's Institutes. She also has introduced Korean cuisine, Chinese cooking and Western cooking through television, radio and magazines and has published several books including the Traditional Korean Cooking Series and Daily Card Menus.

Currently she leads an active life as head of the Munhwa Cooking School and representative director of the Korea Flower Arrangement Society.

About the Copyreader

The English-language copyreader for this cookbook, Shirley A. Dorow, has lived in Seoul, Korea since 1958 with her husband, Maynard W. Dorow, who is a missionary with the Lutheran church. They have four grown children.

During her more than 25 years in Korea Mrs. Dorow's hobby has been cooking with foods from the Korean markets. She has a collection of Korean food slides and has presented several Food Forum slide-talks for newcomers about western-style cooking using Korean market foods. She also wrote a food column for the Korea Times.

Mrs. Dorow is a graduate of Valparaiso University, Valparaiso, Indiana with a B.A. in sociology and religion and has licensure in early childhood education. She taught at Seoul Foreign School for 9½ years.

INTRODUCTION

This cookbook of Korean recipes in English has been prepared for the English reader with the hope that westerner cooks might experience truly authentic Korean dishes. Until now many Korean cookbooks have been presented in English, but they present only those recipes which westerners are presumed to prefer and they modify the recipes for western taste.

This cookbook is authentically Korean. It is a careful translation of recipes prepared by a woman who directs a Korean cooking school in Seoul, Korea for real Korean housewives who are actually using these recipes daily. Even the Korean style layout of the book is the same style as in Korean cookbooks and magazine cooking columns today.

It is true that these recipes stem from age-old Korean traditional recipes and as such are scintillating combinations of food and seasoning unique to the Korean heritage. It is also true, however, that Korean cooking is known for its individual touches. Each family has its own way of seasoning, and brides new to a certain family live with the mother-in-law, even today, long enough to learn these subtle nuances in cooking for their husbands.

The western reader, too, may wish to vary the ingredients according to individual taste. This is acceptable Korean-style cooking. However the recipes presented here present the current vogue based on years of refinement by the collective Korean palate.

Some of these recipes are presented in English for the first time. The step-by-step photo sequences make preparation quite easy and the glossary will help readers understand each individual ingredient and thereby develop a feel for the total impact intended in each recipe.

This book is presented in the hope that gourmet cooks interested in Oriental cookery may extend their repertoire of truly good food and enjoy authentic Korean cooking.

Seoul, Korea
July, 1985

Shirley A. Dorow

PREPARATION TIPS

Korean food preparation methods are quite different from western ones. The main jobs in preparing a Korean meal are the cutting, slicing, seasoning and careful arranging of the food.

The cutting of foods before cooking is very important for appearance as well as convenience in eating with chopsticks. Slicing, chopping, scoring and sectioning the vegetables, fish and meat are techniques employed so that the food will cook quickly and be easier to eat. Also, each ingredient is cut or sliced into the same size or shape and the same thickness so that it cooks evenly and looks neat. Because of the quick cooking the nutritional value remains high as well. Scoring, which is the process of cutting slits in the meat, allows the marinade to penetrate further into meats and also prevents the cooked meat from curling up during cooking. Chopping the seasonings (such as garlic, green onion and ginger) allows for better distribution of the flavor throughout the dish.

Various seasoning sauces are used for marinating meat or fish before broiling or stir-frying. Other sauces are used on vegetables. The amounts of seasonings used may vary with one's preference and other ingredients may also be added to suit one's individual taste.

Some of the sauces are these:

1. Seasoning soy sauce: Combine 4 tbsp. soy sauce, 2 tbsp. sugar, 1 tbsp. rice wine, 1 tbsp. chopped green onion, 1 tbsp. chopped garlic, 1 tbsp. sesame oil, 1 tbsp. sesame salt (crushed sesame that has been toasted with a little salt added), and black pepper to taste. Pine nuts and extra rice wine are optional.

2. Sweet sauce: Combine 1 cup soy sauce, ½ lb. dark corn syrup, ⅓ cup sugar, ⅔ cup water, 1 tbsp. ginger juice or flat slices of fresh ginger, ¼ cup rice wine, 1 tsp. black pepper, and a little MSG in a pan and simmer on low heat until thick.

3. Vinegar-soy sauce: Combine 4 tbsp. soy sauce, 1 tsp. sugar, ½ tbsp. sesame salt, 2 tsp. vinegar, chopped green onion and garlic to taste.

4. Mustard-vinegar sauce: Slowly stir ½ cup boiling water into 7 tbsp. mustard powder; stir until a smooth paste forms in the bowl. Put the bowl containing the mustard paste upside down on a hot cooking pot (perhaps one where rice is cooking) and let it stand for 10-15 minutes. When the mustard is somewhat translucent add 1 tbsp. soy sauce, 3 tbsp. sugar, ½ cup vinegar and 1 tsp. salt and mix well.

5. Seasoned red pepper paste: Combine 2 tbsp. red pepper paste, 2 tbsp. soy sauce, 1 tbsp. chopped garlic, 2 tbsp. chopped green onion, 1 tbsp. sugar, 1 tbsp. sesame salt, and 2 tbsp. sesame oil in a pan and simmer on low heat until thick.

The final step in preparing most dishes is the careful arranging of the foods paying particular attention to alternating the natural colors of the foods to make a pleasant pattern. Foods are always arranged neatly in concentric circles, radial designs or parallel linear columns and never placed in a disorderly fashion. The dish must have eye appeal when presented for eating and recipes often give directions for the exact arrangement of the foods. The photos illustrate this important part of Korean cookery clearly as well.

The recipes in this book will generally serve 4-6 persons.

In the recipes in this book quantities are given in American standard cup and spoon measurements and metric measure for weight.

THE KOREAN DIET

For centuries the Koreans have eaten the fruits of the sea, the field and the mountain because these are the geographically significant features of the Korean peninsula.

The Yellow Sea and Sea of Japan offer excellent fish, seaweed and shellfish for the Korean table. The lowland fields produce excellent grains and vegetables while the uplands grow marvelous fruits and nuts—apple, pear, plum, chestnut, walnut, pine nut and persimmon to name a few. And the ever-present mountains offer wild and cultivated mushrooms, roots and greens. A temperate climate makes for four seasons with the fall harvest being the most abundant. Through the centuries the basic seasonings—red pepper, green onion, soy sauce, bean pastes, garlic, ginger, sesame, mustard, vinegar and wines—have been combined various ways to enhance the meats, fish, seafood and vegetables in the peculiarly spicy and delicious Korean manner. Various regions of Korea have special seasoning combinations—some hotter, some spicier—and each family also has its particular seasoning pattern. One family uses no salted shrimp juice in kimchi; another uses a great deal, but both claim kimchi as an integral part of their daily diet.

Kimchi is a kind of a spicy fermented pickle and accompanies every Korean meal. It is made from cabbage, turnip, cucumber or seasonable vegetables, seasoned with red pepper, garlic, onion, ginger, salt, oysters and soused salted fish juice, and fermented in an earthenware crock. Kimchi is made in large quantities in late autumn for use during the winter months. Autumn kimchi making is called kimjang which is one of Korea's most important household events. Kimchi contains good amounts of vitamin C and stimulates the appetite. Somehow, kimchi and rice make an excellent flavor and texture combination.

The basic diet includes at each meal steamed rice, hot soup, kimchis and a number of meat and/or vegetable side dishes with fruit as an after-meal refresher. In-season fresh vegetables are used at the peak of their season and dried or preserved for out-of-season use later on.

Korean table settings are classified into the 3-chop, the 5-chop, the 7-chop, the 9-chop and the 12-chop setting according to the number of side dishes served. The average family takes three or four side dishes along with rice, soup and kimchi for an everyday Korean meal.

When a family entertains guests for a special occasion, such as a wedding celebration or 60th birthday party, a dozen or more delightful dishes of different kinds are served according to the season. In addition, there is a characteristic way of setting the table for each occasion: New Year's Day Table, Moon-Festival Day Table, Baby's First Birthday Table, Ancestor-Memorial Day Table, Bride's Gift Table or Drinking Table.

Korean food is usually shared by diners. Each person has his own bowl of rice and soup, but other dishes are set on the table for all to reach. The main dishes and the side dishes are distinguished by the quantities served. At meal time, the smaller quantity of the food served will be one of the side dishes. Larger quantity dishes will be the main dish and nothing more will be needed except rice and kimchi.

As for the serving, all the food dishes except hot soups are set at one time on a low table that is set on the floor; at which one sits to eat. The main dishes and the side dishes which are shared by all are placed in the middle of the table. The rice and soup are placed in front of each diner. Chopsticks and spoons are used for eating.

In general the Korean diet is high in grains and vegetables which add much fiber to the diet, moderate but adequate in protein, both animal and vegetable (bean curd, bean sprouts, bean pastes, soy bean sauce), moderate in calories and low in fat and sugar. In short—a very healthy, well-balanced diet. It may be a bit high in salt if soy sauce is used heavily. It may or may not be red peppery hot; it is a matter of individual taste.

The Korean diet is changing and developing but basically the diet pattern has remained the same. Westerners may do well to examine this diet pattern and shift to a similar diet pattern for their own long and healthy life.

Soups
Boiled Main Dishes
Stews
Simmered Mixed Dishes

Clear Fish Soup
Saengsŏn Malgŭnjangkuk (생선 맑은장국)

Ingredients   1 yellow corvina, 2 oz. beef, 1½ tbsp. soy sauce, ½ tbsp. chopped garlic, ½ tsp. sesame oil, black pepper, 3½ cup water, 1 egg, garland chrysanthemum, 3 small green onions

Method   **1** Buy yellow corvina and cut it into several large pieces.
2 Slice the beef cutting against the grain. Season and fry it. Simmer the fried beef with the water to make the meat broth.
3 When the broth boils, add the corvina pieces and bring to a boil again.
4 When the corvina is cooked, check the seasoning and add the sliced small green onion and beaten egg. Add the leaves of garland chrysanthemum just before serving.

Hint   Use chopsticks to hold back the beaten egg so you can pour it slowly into the broth.

1 Cut the corvina into pieces.

2 Boil the beef and then add the corvina.

3 When the corvina is cooked, season and slowly add the beaten egg.

Cold Seaweed and Cucumber Soup
Miyŏk Oinaengkuk (미역 오이냉국)

Ingredients ¼ lb. cucumber, ½ strip brown seaweed, 1½ cup water, 1 tsp. vinegar, 1 tsp. sugar, 1 tsp. soy sauce, 2 tsp. salt, ⅓ green onion, 1 red pepper, ice, MSG

Method **1** Cut the cucumber into thin strips.

2 Soak and clean the seaweed in water. Scald slightly in boiling water and rinse it in cold water. Cut it at ⅓″ intervals.

3 Pour the water into a bowl and sprinkle in the vinegar, sugar and salt. Add the cucumber, seaweed, red pepper strips and ice and serve.

Hint **1** If you add thinly sliced tomato, it becomes "cold tomato soup".

2 Be sure to boil the water first and then use it after it is cooled.

1 Cut the cucumber into thin strips.

3 Season the water with the vinegar, sugar and salt.

2 Scald the soaked seaweed in boiling water and cut.

4 Add the #1 and #2 ingredients to #3.

Croaker Pepper-Pot Soup
Minŏ Maeunťang (민어 매운탕)

1 Scale the croaker and cut it into several large pieces.

2 Cut the carrot and radish into flower-like shapes.

3 When the soup boils, add the fish pieces.

4 When the soup boils again, add the remaining ingredients.

Ingredients 1 croaker, ¼ lb. beef, 1 zucchini, 2 tbsp. red pepper paste, 1 tsp. sesame oil, 1 tsp. red pepper powder, 2 cloves garlic, black pepper, sesame salt, 10 sea mussels, red pepper, green pepper, 3 cups rice water, green onion, 1 piece radish, 1 piece carrot

Method **1** Cut the croaker into several large pieces.
2 Slice the beef thinly and pound it with the back of the knife to tenderize. Season it with the red pepper paste, sesame oil, red pepper powder, garlic, black pepper and sesame salt.
3 Wash the sea mussels in salt water. Cut the zucchini, green pepper and red pepper into large pieces.
4 Stir-fry the seasoned beef and squash in a pan, add the rice water and bring to a boil.
5 When the soup boils, add the fish, flower-shaped carrot and radish pieces and boil again. Then add the sea mussels, green pepper, red pepper, and green onion and bring to a boil once more.

Hint **1** You may use corvina or pollack instead of the croaker according to the season.
2 Croaker tastes better in summer during the breeding season and it may be used then for raw fish or fried fish dishes.

Bellflower Root Soup
Saengch'ot'ang (생초탕)

Ingredients 3 oz. ground beef, ¼ lb. bellflower roots, various seasoning, 2 oz. beef, 1 round onion, 3 dried brown, oak mushrooms, 2 eggs, ½ bundle garland chrysanthemum, 1 tbsp. flour, 1 tbsp. red pepper paste, 2 tsp. salt, 3 cups water, 1 tsp. chopped green onion, 1 tsp. chopped garlic, sesame salt, sesame oil, 1 red pepper, MSG

Method **1** Trim the bellflower roots and rub them well with salt.

2 Wash the bellflower roots and drain. Shred thinly and chop a little.

3 Mix the bellflower roots and ground beef with the flour and beaten egg and season.

4 Slice 2 oz. of beef in flat pieces, season and fry. Then add the sliced dried mushrooms, round onion, and water to this beef and bring it all to a boil.

5 Shape the **#3** mixture into meatballs 1¼" in diameter. Dip them into the beaten egg and drop them into the **#4** boiling soup.

6 When the meatballs have risen to the top, add sliced red pepper or leaves of garland chrysanthemum.

Hint You may add some more red pepper paste to the hot soup.

3 Fry the beef pieces and then add the sliced round onion, dried mushrooms and water and boil.

4 When the soup boils, add the meatballs dipped into the beaten egg.

1 Trim the bellflower roots and shred them finely using a toothpick.

2 Mix the ground beef and bellflower roots with the flour and beaten egg and season.

Hot Pollack Soup
Tongt'aetchigae (동태찌개)

Ingredients   2 pollack, ¼ lb. beef, ½ zucchini, 2 tbsp. red pepper paste, 2 cloves garlic, 3 cups rice water, 4 dried brown, oak mushrooms, 1 large green onion, 3 leaves of garland chrysanthemum, ½ cake bean curd, red pepper, green pepper, ¼ lb. clam, 1 tbsp. soy sauce, 1 tsp. sesame oil, sesame salt

Method   **1** Trim the pollack and cut it into three or four pieces.
2 Cut the zucchini into half-circles. Cut the red peppers, green peppers and large green onion diagonally.
3 Soak the dried mushrooms in water and slice. Cut the bean curd into bite-sized squares.
4 Slice the beef in flat pieces cutting against the grain. Mix the beef, dried mushrooms and zucchini slices with the soy sauce, red pepper paste, sesame salt, garlic and sesame oil. Then fry the mixture lightly in a pot, add the rice water and boil.
5 When the beef broth is fully flavored, add the ground red pepper to the soup.
6 When the soup boils, add the pollack, large green onion and green pepper and bring to a boil again.
7 Add the clams and bean curd pieces to the soup and boil. Add the garland chrysanthemum just before taking the pot off the fire.
Hint   In this simmered dish it is customary to add the clams after the other ingredients are cooked.

1 Trim the pollack and cut it into three or four pieces.

2 Slice the beef and fry it with the seasonings.

3 Add the rice water to **#2** and boil. Then add the zucchini, dried mushroom and ground red pepper.

4 Add the pollack to **#3** and boil. Last of all add the clams and bean curd pieces and boil once more.

Crab Pot-Stew
Kkotketchigae (꽃게찌개)

Ingredients 3 red crabs, ⅓ lb. beef, 1 cake bean curd, 1 egg, 1 large green onion, 1 tsp. sesame oil, 2 tbsp. chopped green onion, 1 tbsp. chopped garlic, salt, black pepper, 1 tbsp. red pepper paste, 1 tbsp. soybean paste, 1 tbsp. red pepper powder, 1 red pepper

Method 1 Scrub the crabs clean with a brush.
2 Open the crabs by splitting them between the top and bottom shell. Cut off the legs and remove all the crab meat with a spoon.
3 Season the crab meat, minced beef and mashed bean curd with the sesame oil, green onion, chopped garlic, salt and black pepper. Add the beaten egg.
4 Dip the top shell of the crab into flour and stuff it with the **#3** mixture. Dip the stuffed crab shell into flour and then into beaten egg and fry lightly in a fry pan.
5 Slice the large green onion diagonally. Dissolve the red pepper paste, soybean paste and red pepper powder in water in a pot and bring to a boil. When it boils, add the crab, large green onion, chopped green onion, red pepper and garlic and check the seasoning.

1 Remove the crab meat from the crab shell.

2 Mix the crab meat, bean curd and beef together.

3 Stuff the top shell of the crab with the **#2** mixture.

4 Fry the stuffed crab shell lightly in a fry pan.

5 When the broth boils, add the fried crab and boil again.

15

Spicy Dried Pollack Stew
Pugŏ Koch'ujangtchigae (북어 고추장찌개)

Ingredients 2 dried pollack, 1/3 lb. bean sprouts, 3 tbsp. red pepper paste, green onion, garlic, 2 green peppers, 2 red peppers, 1 tsp. salt, 3 cup water

Method **1** Pound and soak the dried pollack in water until tender. Remove the flesh from the bones and cut it into pieces 2" long.

2 Dissolve the red pepper paste in the water, add the dried pollack pieces and bring to a boil.

3 Add the trimmed bean sprouts, chopped garlic and sliced green onion and season them with salt.

4 Top the soup with the red pepper and green pepper cut into rings.

Hint Simmer the softened dried pollack until tender. Then add the bean sprouts.

1 Cut the softened pollack into pieces 2" long.

3 When the dried pollack becomes soft, add the trimmed bean sprouts.

2 Add the dried pollack pieces to the boiling broth.

4 Add the sliced green onion and season the soup with salt.

16

Red Snapper Hot Pot
Tomi Chŏn-gol (도미 전골)

Ingredients 1 red snapper, ⅓ lb. beef, 2 large green onions, 2 oz. radish, ½ carrot, ½ bundle watercress, ½ bundle garland chrysanthemum, 20 gingko nuts, 1 red pepper, ½ round onion, 6 dried brown, oak mushrooms, 1 oz. konyak: jellied potato-cake, salt, black pepper, MSG, 3 cups meat stock, 3 tbsp. soy sauce, 1 tbsp. garlic, 1 tbsp. sesame salt, 2 tbsp. cornstarch powder, black pepper

Method 1 Scale the red snapper and remove the entrails through the gills. Clean and make diagonal slits on the red snapper.
2 Sprinkle the salt and black pepper in the slits. Dust the slits with cornstarch powder.
3 Mix the beef, round onion, red pepper, green onion and chopped garlic with the seasoning. Stuff the slits with this mixture.
4 Soak the dried mushrooms in water until soft, remove the stems and cut them into large pieces.
5 Halve the radish trimming the edges into a flower-petal design. Cut the carrot into flowerlike shapes and the watercress into 2⅓″ lengths.
6 Cut the jellied potato-cake into pieces ¾″ × 2⅓″ long and ⅛″ thick. Slit the center, leaving the ends intact and pull one end through the slit forming the same shape as maejagwa, thin Korean cookies.
7 Cut the large green onion diagonally and the garland chrysanthemum into 2⅓″ lengths.
8 Fry the shelled ginko nuts with salt, peel off the skins and cut them into halves.
9 Fry the beef and sliced round onion in a pot and add the broth. When the broth boils, add the red snapper and arrange all the prepared ingredients around the fish attractively. Garnish with the gingko nuts.

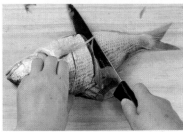

1 Scale off the red snapper and remove the entrails. Slit the fish diagonally.

2 Sprinkle the slits with the salt and black pepper and then the cornstarch powder.

3 Stuff the slits with the seasoned beef, round onion and red pepper mixture.

4 Halve the radish and cut it into thin flowerlike shapes.

Octopus Hot Pot
Nakchi Chŏn-gol (낙지 전골)

Ingredients   2 octopuses, ¼ lb. cabbage, 3 oz. spinach, ½ lb. corbicula clam, 1 cake bean curd, 1 large green onion, 1 Korean green pepper, 1 red pepper, 2 tbsp. rice wine, 3 dried brown, oak mushrooms, 1 round onion, 3 cups meat stock, various seasoning

Method   **1** Clean and cut the octopuses into 2⅓″ long pieces.
2 Parboil the cabbage starting with the stems.

3 Parboil the spinach and mix it with the soy sauce, sesame oil, sugar and salt. Squeeze out the water and wrap it in the scalded cabbage leaf. Cut the rolls into 1¼" lengths.
4 Cut the bean curd into flat pieces ⅓" thick. Cut the green onion into 2" diagonal strips.
5 Soak the clam in salt water overnight and let it stand to remove the sediment.
6 Season the octopus pieces with the red pepper paste, red pepper powder and seasoning. Arrange the prepared ingredients attractively in a casserole.
7 Add the boiling broth to the #6 ingredients, season with salt and bring to a quick boil for the best taste. Serve at once.

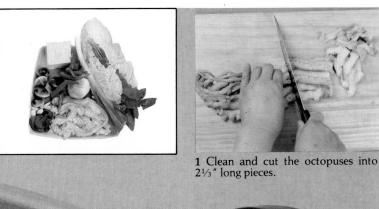

1 Clean and cut the octopuses into 2⅓" long pieces.

2 Place the spinach on the cabbage leaf and roll it up.

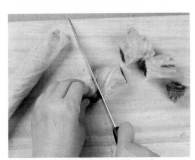

3 Cut the rolls into 1¼" lengths.

4 Cut the bean curd into ¼" thick pieces and the green onion into 2" diagonal strips.

5 Arrange the prepared ingredients in a casserole and add the seasoned octopus pieces.

Vegetable Hot Pot
Yach'ae Chŏn-gol (야채 전골)

Ingredients ⅔ lb. beef, ¼ lb. konyak: jellied potato-cake, ½ zucchini, ⅓ carrot, 10 pine mushrooms, 1 round onion, 1 large green onion, 3 cabbage leaves, ¼ lb. bean sprouts, 2 tbsp. chopped green onion, 2 tbsp. garlic, ½ tsp. sesame oil, 3 tbsp. soy sauce, 1 tbsp. salt, 1 tbsp. red pepper powder, black pepper, MSG, 5 cups water, ½ bundle garland chrysanthemum

Method **1** Slice the beef into thin strips and season it with the soy sauce, green onion, garlic, sugar, sesame oil and MSG.

2 Cut the jellied potato-cake into ¾″ × 2⅓″ pieces. Slit the center leaving the ends intact and pull one end of each piece through the slit.

3 Slice the zucchini and carrot into half-circles.

4 Peel and slice the pine mushrooms. Cut the round onion and cabbage into thick strips.

5 Cut the large green onion diagonally.

6 Arrange the prepared ingredients attractively in a cooking dish. Place the bean sprouts in the center and top them with the pine mushroom slices. Add the seasoned broth and boil briefly at the table.

3 Peel and slice the pine mushrooms.

4 Slice the squash and carrot into half-circles.

1 Cut the beef into thin strips and season.

2 Shape the jellied potato-cake pieces into the same form as maejagwa.

5 Cut the vegetables into thick strips.

20

Steamed Dishes
Stir-Fried Dishes
Soy-Sauce Glazed Dishes

Steamed Red Snapper
Tomitchim (도미찜)

Ingredients 1 red snapper, 1 tsp. salt, black pepper, 2 oz. beef, ½ cake bean curd, green onion, garlic, sesame oil, ½ tsp. salt, ½ tsp. sesame salt, 1 tsp. soy sauce, ½ cucumber, ½ carrot, 3 dried brown, oak mushrooms, 2 eggs, 10 quail eggs, ½ tomato, ½ bundle parsley, pine nuts, lemon

Method **1** Clean and scale the red snapper. Fillet the fish keeping the skeleton and head intact. Slice the fish fillets into bite-sized pieces and sprinkle them with the salt and black pepper.

2 Chop the beef finely. Squeeze out the water from the bean curd. Mix the beef and bean curd with the soy sauce, green onion, garlic, sesame oil and sesame salt.

3 Cut the cucumber into thin strips and sprinkle it with salt. Squeeze out the water and fry lightly.

4 Soak the dried mushrooms and cut them into thin strips. Sprinkle them with the soy sauce and sugar and fry.

5 Cut the carrot into thin strips and sprinkle it with salt and fry. Fry the egg white and egg yolk separately into sheets and cut them into thin strips.

6 Dip the red snapper slices into flour. Wrap the beef and pine nut in the fish slice and roll. Then dip the rolls into beaten egg and fry until brown.

7 Place the fried fish rolls on the fish skeleton. Cover with the vegetables alternating colors. Steam the stuffed red snapper on a steamer rack until tender for 10-15 minutes.

8 Boil and peel the quail eggs and cut them in half. Garnish with the quail egg, tomato and parsley.

Hint **1** When serving the whole red snapper, place the head of the red snapper at the left of the plate.

2 If the plate has too much liquid in it after steaming the fish, remove the fish to a dry plate.

3 Cut the cucumber, dried mushrooms and carrot into thin strips and fry them separately.

1 Clean and scale the red snapper. Fillet the fish.

4 Cut the two fillets into bite-sized pieces. Place the #2 mixture and pine nuts on the fish slice and roll.

2 Chop the beef finely. Squeeze out the water from the bean curd and season.

5 Dip the rolls into flour and egg and fry until brown.

Steamed Ark Shell Clams
Komaktchim (고막찜)

Ingredients 3 cups ark shell clams, 4 tbsp. soy sauce, ½ tbsp. sugar, 1 tbsp. red pepper powder, 2 tbsp. chopped garlic, 4 tbsp. chopped green onion, 2 tbsp. sesame salt, 1 tbsp. sesame oil, red pepper thread, pine nuts, lettuce

Method **1** Clean the ark shell clams by rubbing them with salt and soak them in salt water so that the clams will spit out the watery sediment; drain.

2 Mix the soy sauce, chopped green onion, garlic, red pepper thread, red pepper powder, sesame salt, black pepper and sesame oil to make the seasoning sauce.

3 Scald the ark shells or steam them in a steamer. Remove one side of the shell and the organs from the clam meat. Re-place the meat in the shells, sprinkle with the seasoning sauce and top them with the pine nut.

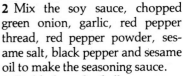

1 Clean the ark shells and scald them in boiling water.

3 Remove the organ from the ark shell neatly.

6 Place the fried rolls on the skeleton.

2 Remove one side of the shell, leaving the other side to which the flesh is attached.

4 Sprinkle the seasoning sauce on the clam meat.

7 Top the skeleton with the prepared vegetables alternating colors.

8 Steam on a rack in the steamer for 10-15 minutes.

Steamed Abalones
Chonboktchim 〔전복찜〕

Ingredients 6 abalones, 3 walnuts, 6 gingko nuts, 3 tbsp. soy sauce, 1½ tbsp. sugar, 1 tbsp. rice wine, 3 cloves garlic, 1 knob ginger, black pepper, sesame oil, ½ cup water, 2 cups green sweet peas, radish, parsley

Method **1** Clean the abalones and scald in boiling salted water.
2 Remove the shells and entrails from the abalones. Score the insides at ¼" intervals crosswise and lengthwise.
3 Soak the walnuts in hot water and peel off the inner skin using a toothpick.

4 Fry the shelled ginko nuts with salt until the color becomes green; rub off the skins.
5 Boil the seasoning sauce in a pan, add the abalones and simmer.
6 On a skewer, string the gingko nut, abalone and walnut alternately. Place the skewered food on the shell of the abalone.
7 Boil the green peas in salted water and stir-fry lightly. Spread them on a plate and arrange the abalone in the shells on top. Garnish with the red radish and parsley.

3 Score the insides of the abalones.

4 Peel the inner skin off the walnuts using a toothpick.

1 Clean the abalones and scald them in boiling water.

2 Remove the shells and entrails from the abalones and clean.

5 Add the abalones to the boiling seasoning sauce and simmer.

24

Steamed Stuffed Clams
Taehaptchim (대합찜)

Ingredients   **A.** 4 large clams, 2 oz. beef, ½ cake bean curd, 1 egg, ¼ tsp. salt, 1 tsp. sesame salt, 1 tsp. sesame oil, green onion, garlic, black pepper
B. 1 egg, ½ bundle parsley, 2 cups coarse salt
Method   1 Soak the large clams in water overnight, so that they spit out the sand and watery sediment.
2 Clean the clams and scald them in boiling water. Remove the clam meat from the shell and chop it finely. Clean the shells and set aside.
3 Fry the chopped beef lightly in a greased pan and chop it finely again. Fry the beaten egg yolk and white separately into thin sheets.
4 Squeeze out the excess water from the bean curd and mash.
5 Mix the chopped clam meat, beef, beaten egg and bean curd with the **A** seasonings. Fill the trimmed shells with the mixture and garnish them with fine strips of the cooked egg white and yolk and parsley.
6 Place the stuffed shells on a steamer rack in the steamer and steam for 10 minutes. Arrange the steamed stuffed clams on coarse salt on a plate.

1 Scald the large clams in boiling water.

3 Chop the beef and the clam meat.

5 Season the chopped beef, clam meat and mashed bean curd.

2 Chop the beef finely and fry.

4 Fry the beaten egg yolk and white separately.

6 Fill the clam shells with the #5 mixture and garnish.

25

Steamed Stuffed Crabs
Ketchim (게찜)

Ingredients   3 red crabs, ¼ lb. beef, 1 cake bean curd, 2 eggs, 1 large green onion, 4 cloves garlic, ½ tsp. sesame oil, 1 tsp salt, black pepper, 3 stone mushrooms, red pepper thread, lettuce, parsley

Method   1 Scrub the crabs with salt and clean. Leaving the large legs intact, remove the bottom shells and small legs from the crabs. Remove the crab meat from the shells and place it in a bowl.

2 Mince the beef finely; squeeze out the water from the bean curd.

3 Combine the crab meat, minced beef, bean curd, green onion, garlic, egg, sesame oil, salt and black pepper.

4 Soak the stone mushrooms in water and cut them into thin strips. Fry the beaten egg yolk and white into sheets separately and cut them into thin strips.

5 Grease the insides of the crab shells and fill with the **#3** mixture. Top them with the stone mushroom, egg strips and red pepper threads and steam with the large legs in a steamer. Garnish with the parsley on lettuce on a plate.

1 Remove the bottom shells and legs from the crabs.

2 Remove the crab meat from the shells.

3 Season the crab meat, beef and bean curd.

4 Fill the crab shells with the **#3** mixture.

5 Steam the stuffed crabs and legs in a steamer.

26

Steamed Conches
Soratchim (소라찜)

Ingredients 6 Top-shell, 1 egg, ½ bundle parsley, 1 red pepper, sesame oil, salt, 3 boiled ears of corn, 2 stone mushrooms

Method **1** Clean and steam the Top-shell in a steamer.

2 Fry the beaten egg yolk and white separately into sheets and cut them into thin strips.

3 Remove the seeds from the red pepper and cut it into short, thin strips. Chop the parsley finely.

4 Soak the stone mushrooms in water and cut them into thin strips.

5 Take the meat out of the boiled Top-shell and remove the entrails. Slice thinly and mix with the salt and sesame oil.

6 Fill the shells with the seasoned Top-shell meat and garnish with the egg and vegetable strips.

7 Place the fried boiled corn on a plate and place the stuffed conches on the corn. Garnish with the parsley.

Hint When you steam the food, add the food to the steamer after the water boils. The inside of the steamer and the food get wet if you add the food to the steamer when the temperature is too low.

3 Take the Top-shell meat out of the shells and slice thinly; season it with the salt and sesame oil.

4 Fill the Top-shell with the seasoned meat and garnish.

1 Clean and steam the Top-shell in a steamer.

2 Chop the parsley finely. Cut the egg sheets and vegetables into thin strips.

Steamed Stuffed Eggplant
Kajitchim (가지찜)

Ingredients 3 eggplants, salt, 2 oz. beef, ½ cake bean curd, 1 round onion, ½ green onion, 1 clove garlic, 1 tbsp. red pepper paste, 1 tbsp. soy sauce, 1 tbsp. sesame salt, black pepper, MSG, 1 tbsp. sesame oil, ½ cup meat stock

Method 1 Halve small sleek eggplant. Slit each piece twice through the middle, with the two cuts at right angles leaving the ends intact. Soak them in salt water and then squeeze out the water.

2 Mince the beef finely and squeeze out the excess water from the bean curd. Mix the seasoning with the beef and bean curd. Stuff the slits with the mixture.

3 Place the stuffed eggplants on a layer of sliced round onions in a pot. Add the meat stock and simmer; or steam in a steamer.

1 Cut the scalded cabbage leaves and vegetables into thin strips.

2 Season the vegetables well with the salt, black pepper and sesame oil.

1 Halve the eggplants, and slit each piece at right angles.

2 Stuff the slits with the seasoned mashed bean curd and minced beef.

3 Place the stuffed eggplants on a layer of the sliced round onion in a pot and simmer.

Steamed Cabbage and Vegetables
Yangbaech'u Yach'aetchim (양배추 야채찜)

3 Sprinkle the **#2** vegetables with some flour and mix them into the thick dough.

4 Shape the dough into a square patty and steam in a steamer.

5 Scald the green beans in salt water. Fry in butter and wrap them firmly in the sheet of laver.

Ingredients   ⅓ lb. cabbage, 2 oz. beef, ½ round onion, 2 oz. bracken, 2 oz. bellflower roots,3 dried brown, oak mushrooms, 3 Korean green peppers, 1 red pepper, 2 oz. carrot, 2 cups flour, ½ cup water, 2 tsp. salt, black pepper, sesame oil, laver, long green beans, vinegar-soy sauce: (4 tbsp. soy sauce, green onion, garlic, sesame salt, 1 tsp. sugar, 2 tsp vinegar.)

Method   **1** Remove the thick veins from the cabbage. Scald the cabbage and cut it into thin strips. **2** Slice the beef into thin strips and season. Soak the dried mushrooms in water and remove the stems. Slice them into thin strips. **3** Parboil the bracken and bellflower roots and cut them into 2" lengths. Cut the carrot into thin strips and scald.
4 Halve the green peppers and red pepper and remove the seeds. Cut them into thick strips.
5 Season the vegetable strips with the salt, black pepper, MSG and sesame oil and sprinkle them with the flour.
6 Knead the flour with water to make a thick dough. Then mix the dough with the **#7** seasoned vegetables.
7 Shape the **#8** mixture into a square patty and steam it in a damp cloth in the steamer.
8 Cut the cooled steamed patty into bite-sized pieces. Scald the green beans and stir-fry lightly. Wrap them in the sheet of laver and cut diagonally. Arrange the steamed vegetable pieces and green bean bundles on a plate. Serve with vinegar-soy sauce.

Steamed Stuffed Fish
Ŏsŏn (어선)

Ingredients   1 pollack, ½ bundle watercress, ¼ lb. carrot, 6 dried brown, oak mushrooms, 2 eggs, 1 tbsp. salt, 5 tbsp. cornstarch powder, 4 cabbage leaves, 1 tsp. sesame oil, 1 tomato, parsley, 3 tbsp. soy sauce, 1 tsp. vinegar, 1 tsp. pine nut

Method   1 Slice the pollack thinly and sprinkle with the salt and black pepper.

2 Trim and clean the watercress. Stir-fry the stems mixing them with the salt and sesame oil.

3 Soak the dried mushrooms in water, squeeze out the water. Cut them into thin strips and season them with the soy sauce, sugar, and sesame oil and fry.

4 Cut the carrot into thin strips and fry sprinkling with salt.

5 Fry the beaten egg yolk and white separately into sheets and cut them into thin strips.

6 Dip the pollack slices into the cornstarch powder. Place the watercress, carrot, dried mushroom and egg strips on each fish slice and wrap the fish around them firmly.

7 Place the #6 rolls on a damp cloth in a steamer and steam. Cool the steamed rolls and cut them into 1⅔" lengths.

8 Mix the soy sauce, vinegar and chopped pine nuts to make the vinegar-soy sauce.

9 Place a layer of shredded cabbage on a plate and arrange the sliced fish rolls attractively. Garnish with the tomato and parsley. Serve with vinegar-soy sauce for dipping.

1 Slice the pollack thinly and sprinkle with the salt and black pepper.

2 Fry the watercress, carrot and dried mushrooms separately.

3 Place the vegetable and egg strips on the pollack slice dipped into the starch powder, and wrap them firmly.

Stuffed Zucchini
Hobaksŏn (호박선)

Ingredients 2 young zucchini, ¼ lb. beef, 1 tsp. sesame salt, 2 tsp. soy sauce, ½ tsp. salt, 1 tsp. sesame oil, black pepper, 2 tsp. chopped garlic 1 tbsp. chopped green onion, 3 dried brown, oak mushrooms, 1 egg, 1 round onion, 1 cup meat stock, 1 stone mushroom, pine nuts, salt, red pepper thread

Method 1 Choose tender, straight zucchini and cut them into 2″ lengths. Put X slits on the zucchini chunks and sprinkle them with salt.

4 Steam the rolls on a damp cloth in a steamer.

2 Soak the dried mushrooms in water to soften and remove the stems. Cut them into thin strips.

3 Combine the minced beef, dried mushroom strips, sesame salt, soy sauce, salt, sesame oil, black pepper, chopped green onion and garlic.

4 Halve the round onion and cut it into thin strips.

5 Fry the beaten egg yolk and white separately into thin sheets and cut them into thin strips.

6 Stuff the squash with the egg strips and red pepper thread.

7 Place the stuffed squash chunks on a layer of sliced round onion in a pot.

8 Add 1 cup of meat broth seasoned with the soy sauce, salt and black pepper and bring to a boil.

Hint In order not to cut the zucchini too far, place the zucchini pieces between two wooden chopsticks. They will stop the knife before it cuts all the way through the zucchini.

1 Put X slits in the zucchini chunks placed between two chopsticks.

2 Sprinkle the zucchini chunks with salt.

3 Stuff the slits with the seasoned beef.

4 Place the stuffed zucchini chunks on a layer of sliced round onion in a pot.

Fried Octopus
Nakchibokkŭm (낙지볶음)

2 Rub the octopus pieces with salt and rinse clean.

4 When the garlic is cooked, add the round onion, carrot and the seasoned red pepper paste.

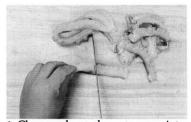

1 Clean and cut the octopuses into 2⅓" lengths.

3 Cut the carrot, round onions and green peppers into rectangular pieces.

5 Fry the octopus pieces with the #4 mixture and sprinkle the sesame oil and sesame seed last of all.

Ingredients   3 octopuses, 1 green onion, 2 round onions, ½ carrot, black pepper, 1 tbsp. sugar, 3 tbsp. red pepper paste, 2 tbsp. red pepper powder, 2 tbsp. soy sauce, MSG, ginger juice, green onion, garlic, sesame oil, sesame seed, Korean green peppers

Method   **1** Rub the octopuses with salt and rinse clean. Cut them into 2⅓" lengths.

2 Remove the seeds from the green peppers. Cut them and the carrot into rectangles. Halve the round onions and slice them the same size as the carrot pieces.

3 Slice the garlic; cut the green onion diagonally.

4 Fry the garlic, carrot and round onion lightly in an oiled pan; add the red pepper paste, red pepper powder, soy sauce, sugar, green onion, green pepper and octopus pieces and continue to fry. When done, sprinkle on the sesame oil and sesame seed and mix well.

Hint   You may rub the octopuses with salt to clean them after cutting them into pieces.

32

Fried Young Squash
Aehobakpokkŭm (애호박볶음)

Ingredients   1 young squash (zucchini), 2 oz. beef, 1 large green onion, 4 cloves garlic, 2 tsp. sesame salt, 2 tsp. sesame oil, 2 tbsp. soused salted shrimp juice, soy sauce, red pepper thread, salt

Method   **1** Halve the young squash and cut it into half-circle pieces. Sprinkle the squash pieces with salt and let them stand.
2 Slice the beef and season it with the green onion, garlic, sesame salt, sesame oil and soy sauce.
3 Squeeze the water out from the salted squash and stir-fry lightly; place it on a plate.
4 Fry the beef and mix it with the squash pieces, shredded red pepper thread and season it with the salted shrimp juice.

Hint   **1** Fry the young squash separately and add it to the fried beef later for a fresher taste.
2 Fry the squash briefly because it loses its taste if cooked too long.

1 Cut the young squash into half-circle pieces, sprinkle it with salt and let it stand.

3 Squeeze the water out from the squash and fry lightly.

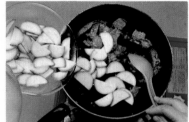

4 After frying the beef, add the squash pieces and fry lightly.

2 Slice the beef and season.

5 Season with the soused salted shrimp juice and red pepper thread.

Stir-Fried Anchovies with Peppers
Putkoch'u Myŏlch'ibokkŭm (풋고추 멸치볶음)

Ingredients ⅓ lb. Korean-style long green peppers, ¼ lb. dried anchovies, 3 tbsp. soy sauce, 2 cloves garlic, 1½ tbsp. sugar, 1 tsp. sesame oil, 2 tbsp. salad oil, sesame seed, red pepper thread

Method **1** Wash the small green peppers and drain. Remove the stems.
2 Trim the small dried anchovies carefully.
3 Slice the garlic.
4 Stir-fry the anchovies and garlic lightly in an oiled pan. Add the soy sauce and sugar and then the green peppers and fry a bit more.
5 When the ingredients are almost cooked, add the sesame oil and red pepper thread and mix well.

Hint **1** Choose small-sized dried anchovies. Fry the green peppers quickly in order to keep the green color.
2 Choose the long Korean peppers (not hot).

1 Fry the dried anchovies and garlic in a greased pan.

2 Add the seasoning and the green peppers to #1 and fry.

3 When the ingredients are almost done, add the sesame oil, sesame seed and red pepper thread and fry.

Sea Mussel in Soy Sauce
Honghapch'o (홍합초)

Ingredients   **A.** ¼ lb. dried sea mussels, 2 oz. beef
B. 5 tbsp. soy sauce, 3 tbsp. sugar, 5 cloves garlic, ½ oz. ginger, 1 cup water
C. sesame seed

Method   **1** Slice the garlic and ginger in thin pieces.
2 Soak the dried sea mussels in water to soften.
3 Simmer the sliced beef and sea mussel seasoned with the garlic, ginger and the **B** ingredients until glazed.
4 Place the **#3** simmered ingredients in a bowl and sprinkle with sesame seed.

1 Slice the garlic and ginger in thin pieces.

2 Slice the beef.

3 Add the **#1**, **#2** ingredients to the sea mussels and simmer.

Abalones in Soy Sauce
Chŏnbokch'o (전복초)

Ingredients 6 abalones, ⅓ cup sweet soy sauce, 2 cabbage leaves, powdered pine nuts, parsley

Method **1** Wash the abalones and scald them in salt water. Remove the shells, entrails and lips of the abalones.

2 Score the trimmed abalones crosswise and lengthwise.

3 Simmer the scored abalones with sweet soy sauce until glazed.

4 Place the simmered abalones in the cleaned shells and sprinkle them with the powdered pine nuts.

5 Arrange the **#4** abalones on shredded cabbage on a plate and garnish with the parsley.

Hint **1** Scald the abalone to make it tender and then remove the meat from the shell.

2 You may place the abalone meat directly on a plate instead of the shells.

1 Wash the abalones and scald in hot water.

2 Remove the shells and organs from the abalones.

3 Score the back side of the abalone meat.

4 Simmer the abalones in the sweet soy sauce.

5 Place the abalone meat in the shells and sprinkle with powdered pine nuts.

Soy-Sauce Glazed Cutlass-Fish
Kalch'ijorim (갈치조림)

Ingredients   1 cutlass-fish, salt, black pepper, ½ white Korean radish, 3 cloves garlic, 1 large green onion, 1 tbsp. red pepper powder, 4 tbsp. soy sauce, 2 tbsp. sugar, 1 knob ginger, ½ cup cornstarch powder, oil

Method   **1** Scrape the skin of the cutlass-fish with the knife and remove the entrails. Wash it and cut it into pieces 2¾″ long. Slit each piece at ¼″ intervals and sprinkle with the salt and black pepper.

2 Cut the radish into pieces 1¼″ long and cut X slit on each piece. Scald in boiling water and drain.

3 Dip the cutlass-fish pieces into the cornstarch powder and deep-fry them in oil.

4 Boil the **#2** radish pieces with the soy sauce, red pepper powder, green onion, garlic, sugar, ginger and water in a pot. When it boils, add the **#3** cutlass-fish pieces and sprinkle with the red pepper powder.

1 Trim and cut the cutlass-fish into pieces 2¾″ long and score them at ¼″ intervals.

2 Dip the cutlass-fish into the cornstarch powder and deep-fry in oil.

3 Put X slits on the radish pieces.

4 Simmer the radish in the seasoning sauce.

5 Add the deep-fried cutlass-fish to **#4** and simmer.

Soy-Sauce Glazed Mackerel Pike Meatballs
Kkongch'iwanjajorim (꽁치완자조림)

Ingredients   2 mackerel pikes, ½ round onion, ½ carrot, 2 cloves garlic, 1 knob ginger, ½ cucumber, ¼ carrot, 3 tbsp. soy sauce, 2 tbsp. red pepper powder, 1 tsp. sugar, ½ tbsp. salt, black pepper, ⅓ cup bread flour, flour, 1 egg, frying oil, 10 skewers

Method   **1** Remove the thick bones and entrails from the mackerel. Rinse, dry and chop finely.
2 Chop the carrot and round onion finely and sprinkle them with salt. Squeeze out the water.
3 Mix the chopped mackerel pike meat, round onion and carrot with the green onion, garlic,

ginger, salt, black pepper and bread flour. Knead and shape the mixture into meatballs ¾″ in diameter. Dip the meatballs into flour and then into beaten egg and deep-fry them in oil.
4 Boil ½ cup of water with the

soy sauce, garlic, ginger, red pepper powder and sugar. Add the meatballs and simmer.
5 String the cucumber and meatballs on skewers and place them on a paper doily on a plate. Garnish with the flower-shaped carrot.

2 Chop the round onion and carrot finely and sprinkle them with salt.

4 Shape the **#3** mixture into meatballs, dip them in flour and then into beaten egg and deep-fry in oil.

1 Remove the mackerel from the bones and rinse.

3 Mix **#1** and **#2** with the bread flour, soy sauce, salt, sugar, green onion and garlic.

5 Add the deep-fried meatballs to the boiling seasoning sauce and simmer.

Soy-Sauce Glazed Burdock Root
Uŏngjorim (우엉조림)

Ingredients   ½ lb. burdock root, ¼ lb. beef, ¼ lb. konyak: jellied potato-cake, ⅔ cup soy sauce, ⅓ cup sugar, ¼ cup rice wine, 1½ cup water, pine nut powder

Method   **1** Peel and scald the burdock root and cut it into thick strips.
2 Cut the beef into ¼″ thick strips.
3 Cut the jellied potato-cake into ¾″×2⅓″ long and ⅛″ thick pieces. Score the center leaving the ends intact and pull one end of each piece through the slits. (Shape each piece into the same form as maejagwa.)
4 Place the beef, burdock root and jellied potato-cake pieces with the seasoning in a pot, cover and simmer. When the liquid is almost evaporated, remove the lid and simmer on high heat until glazed.
5 Place the food in a bowl and sprinkle it with the powdered pine nuts.

1 Peel and cut the burdock root into chunks and then scald it in boiling water.

2 Cut the beef and burdock root into thick strips.

3 Place the beef, burdock root and jellied potato-cake pieces in a pot and simmer until glazed.

Soy-Sauce Glazed Lotus Root
Yŏn-gŭnjorim (연근조림)

Ingredients ⅔ lb. lotus root, ¼ lb. beef, ½ round onion, ½ cup soy sauce, 4 tbsp. black sugar, 4 tbsp. rice wine, 1½ oz. dark corn syrup, 2 tbsp. oil, vinegar, sesame salt, MSG, 2 cups water, radish, parsley

Method **1** Peel the lotus root and slice it into pieces ¼" thick.

2 Sprinkle the sliced lotus root in vinegar, drop in boiling water, remove and trim the edges into flowerlike shapes.

3 Slice the beef. Cut the round onion into pieces ⅓" square.

4 Simmer the sliced lotus root with the seasoning on low heat in an oiled pan.

5 When the #5 seasoning is almost evaporated, add the beef and round onion and simmer on high heat until glazed.

6 Garnish with the red radish and parsley.

Hint In order to keep the sliced lotus root white, you may add salt, vinegar and sugar to it or put it in vinegar-water.

1 Sprinkle the lotus root with vinegar and drop into boiling water.

3 Simmer the lotus root with the seasoning.

2 Trim the edges of the sliced lotus root into flowerlike shapes.

Broiled Foods
Deep-Fried Foods
Skewered Foods
Pan-Fried Foods

Broiled Spanish Mackerel
Samch'i Sogŭmgui (삼치 소금구이)

Ingredients   1 Spanish mackerel, 3 tbsp. salt, ¼ radish, cucumber, lemon, parsley

Method   1 Scale and clean the Spanish mackerel. Remove the entrails. Cut the fish into four pieces and put X slits on both sides.

2 Sprinkle the pieces with the salt and let them stand.

3 Broil the salted fish on a heated oiled grill. When using an oven-broiler, place the fish in a heated pan and broil.

4 Place the broiled fish pieces on a layer of shredded white radish on a plate and garnish with the parsley, lemon and cucumber.

Hint   After scoring the fish pieces, marinate them in the seasoning sauce. Then broil them on a grill, basting the fish with the seasoning sauce.

1 Remove the entrails from the Spanish mackerel. Clean and cut it into pieces.

2 Put X slits on both sides of the pieces.

3 Sprinkle the fish pieces with the salt and let them stand.

4 Broil on a heated oiled grill.

Seasoned Broiled Eel
Changŏ Yangnyŏmgui (장어 양념구이)

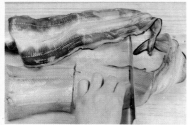

1 Clean the eels and cut them into pieces 4″.

3 Broil the eel pieces on a heated oiled grill.

Ingredients   **A** 2 eels
B 1 tsp. ginger juice, 1½ tbsp. sugar, 1 tbsp. rice wine, 5 tbsp. soy sauce, 3 tbsp. chopped green onion, 1 tbsp. chopped garlic, sesame salt, black pepper, sesame oil, 3 tbsp. water
C 1 cucumber, 1 red pepper

Method   **1** Choose fresh, live eels. Remove the heads and the entrails. Halve and slice the eels.
2 Boil the **B** ingredients slightly to make a thick seasoning sauce.
3 Pound the sliced eels with the tip of the knife and cut them into pieces. Broil the pieces on a heated grill.
4 Baste the eels with the seasoning sauce and broil again.
5 Place the broiled eels in a dish and garnish with the cucumber and red pepper.

2 Boil the **B** ingredients to make the thick seasoning sauce.

4 Baste the eels with the seasoning sauce and broil again.

43

Broiled Squid
Ojingŏgui (오징어구이)

Ingredients   2 squid, 2 tbsp. soy sauce, 2 green onions, 2 tbsp. red pepper paste, ½ tbsp. sugar, 1 tbsp. chopped garlic, ½ tbsp. sesame salt, 2 red peppers, 2 long Korean green peppers, sesame oil, red pepper thread, black pepper, MSG

Method   **1** Halve the fresh squid lengthwise and clean.
2 Flatten the squid and skin it by rubbing it with the salt.
3 Dry and score the inside of the squid crosswise and lengthwise at 1" intervals. Cut it into pieces 1⅔"×2"
4 Scald the squid pieces in boiling water and drain.
5 Make the seasoning sauce with the red pepper paste and soy sauce.
6 Baste the squid pieces with the seasoning sauce and broil the squid on medium heat on a grill.
7 Garnish with the red pepper.

Hint   You can skin the body of the squid by rubbing it with a cloth dipped into salt.

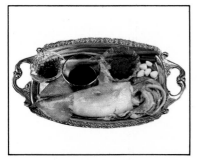

1 Skin the body of the squid.

2 Halve the squid and cut diagonal slits.

4 Scald the squid pieces in boiling water.

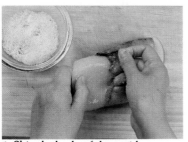

3 Cut the scored squid into bite-sized pieces.

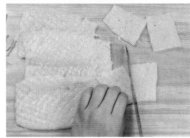

5 Baste with the seasoning sauce and broil on a grill.

44

Seasoned Broiled Corvina
Chogi Yangnyomgui (조기 양념구이)

Ingredients   1 corvina, 2 tbsp. soy sauce, 1 tbsp. vinegar, 1 tbsp. sesame salt, 1 tbsp. chopped green onion, ½ tbsp. garlic, ginger juice, 2 tsp. red pepper powder, 2 tsp. sesame oil, 1 tsp. sugar, black pepper, ½ tomato, lettuce, ¼ cucumber

Method   **1** Select fresh yellow corvina. Clean the corvina removing the entrails and the scales. Wash well and pat dry.

2 Put deep slits on both sides of the fish at ¾″ intervals.

3 Mix the soy sauce with the seasoning to make the seasoning sauce.

4 Baste the corvina with the seasoning sauce and broil it on medium heat on a heated oiled grill until golden-brown.

5 Serve the broiled corvina on a plate with the lettuce leaves, tomato and cucumber.

2 Mix the seasoning to make the seasoning sauce.

1 Clean the fish and score deeply on both sides of the fish at ¾″ intervals.

3 Baste the fish with the seasoning sauce and broil on an oiled grill.

Broiled Trout
Songŏgui (송어구이)

Ingredients 1 trout, 4 tbsp. salt, ½ lemon, soy sauce, rice wine, sugar, lettuce

Method **1** Clean the trout removing the fin and entrails. Divide the fish into half and remove the flesh from the bones.
2 Cut the trout into appropriately sized pieces and put slits through the skin. Sprinkle the fish pieces with the salt and let them stand.
3 When well-salted, broil the fish on a heated oiled grill.
4 Place the broiled fish on lettuce leaves on a plate and garnish with the lemon slices.

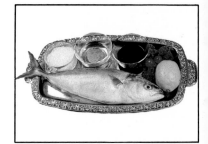

1 Cut through the skin of the fish pieces.

2 Sprinkle the fish pieces with the salt and let them stand.

3 Broil on a heated oiled grill.

1 Remove the head and the shell from the prawn leaving the tail area including the second joint intact.

2 Remove the innards by splitting the back of the prawn and sprinkle with the salt.

3 Shape the beef and bean curd mixture into the meatballs and place one meatball on each prawn.

46

Broiled Prawns
Taehagui (대하구이)

Ingredients   5 prawns, 1 oz. beef, ¼ cake bean curd, salt, black pepper, garlic, sesame oil, sweet soy sauce, radish, parsley, pine nut powder

Method   **1** Remove the head and the shell from the prawns leaving the tail area including the second joint intact. Remove the innards by splitting the back of the prawn and sprinkle with salt.
2 Mince the beef finely. Squeeze out the water from the bean curd and mash.
3 Mix the minced beef and mashed bean curd with the seasoning. Shape the mixture by tablespoonfuls into the oval meatballs. Place each meatball on a prawn.
4 Broil the prawns in a fry pan or an oven-broiler for 10 minutes. Then baste them with sweet soy sauce and broil again.
5 Place the broiled prawns on a layer of shredded white radish on a plate. Sprinkle with the powdered pine nuts and garnish with the parsley.

4 Broil the prawns and the heads for 10 minutes in an oven-broiler.

5 Baste them with sweet soy sauce and broil again.

47

Broiled Todok
Tŏdŏkkui (더덕구이)

Ingredients   15 todoks (a white root), 2 tbsp. red pepper paste, ½ tbsp. red pepper powder, 2 tbsp. soy sauce, 1 tbsp. chopped garlic, 2 tbsp. chopped green onion, 1 tbsp. sugar, 1 tbsp. sesame salt, 2 tbsp. sesame oil, salt

Method   1 After soaking and peeling the todok, remove the bitterness by soaking the todok in salt water; then pat them dry. Slice the todok thinly and pound it flat with a mallet.

2 Mix the red pepper paste with the soy sauce, green onion, garlic, sesame salt and sesame oil. Simmer the mixture until thickened.

3 Broil the todok on a grill and baste it with the seasoned red pepper paste.

1 Remove the bitterness by soaking the todok in salt water.

3 Pound the thinly sliced todok flat with the mallet.

2 Pat the todok dry with a dry cloth.

4 Baste the broiled todok with the seasoned red pepper paste.

48

Deep-Fried Shrimp
Saeut'wigim (새우튀김)

Ingredients   **A** 6 shrimp, 2 eggs, ½ cup flour, salt, black pepper
B ½ cup white sesame seed, ½ cup black sesame seed, ½ cup peanut powder
C ginger juice, 2 tbsp. soy sauce, 1 tbsp. rice wine, 6 tbsp. kelp broth
D lemon, parsley

Method   **1** Prepare fresh, large shrimp by removing the shells from the shrimps leaving the tail area including the second joint intact.
2 Remove the entrails by splitting the back, and cut off the red fibers from the legs. Tenderize the shrimp by pounding them with the back of the knife. Sprinkle the shrimp with the salt and black pepper.

3 Dust the shrimp (except the tail area) evenly with flour.
4 Mix the beaten egg and flour to make a thick paste.
5 Dip the shrimp into the thick paste and then into the black sesame seed, white sesame seed and peanut powder. Deep-fry them in oil at 340°F.
6 Boil the **C** seasonings and remove the froth from the top.
7 Stand the shrimps on end on a plate and garnish with the parsley and lemon. Serve with the #6 seasoning sauce.

Hint   Cut ⅛" from the tail of the shrimp, otherwise the oil may splash and burn you when adding the shrimp to the boiling oil.

1 Trim and score the shrimp at ⅓" intervals.

2 Cut ½ from the tail of the shrimp.

3 Dust the shrimp (except the tail area) with flour.

4 Mix the beaten egg and flour to make a thick paste.

5 Dip the shrimp into the thick paste and then into the black sesame seed and peanut powder and deep-fry.

Deep-Fried Vegetables
Yach'aet'wigim (야채튀김)

Ingredients 1 potato, ½ carrot, 5 sesame leaves, 4 stems garland chrysanthemum, 1 round onion, 1 burdock root, 3 green peppers, 1 cup flour, 1 egg yolk, ⅔ cup ice water, frying oil

Method 1 Peel the potato and cut it into circles ¼″ thick. Wash it in salt water.

2 Trim the sesame leaves and garland chrysanthemum. Slice the round onion into ¼″ thick disks and insert a toothpick through the layers.

3 Cut the carrot into thin strips. Peel and cut the burdock root into pieces. Scald the burdock pieces and cut them into thin strips. Soak them in cold water to remove any discoloration.

4 Score the green peppers slightly.

5 Mix the egg yolk and flour with ⅔ cup ice water to make a thick paste.

6 Dip the prepared vegetables into the thick paste and deep-fry them briefly in oil at 360°F.

1 Cut the potato into ¼″ thick disks and soak it in salt water.

2 Peel the burdock root and soak it in cold water. Cut the burdock root and carrot into thin strips.

3 Cut the round onion into ¼″ thick disks and insert a toothpick through the layers.

4 Score the clean green peppers.

5 Mix the ice water, egg yolk and flour to make a thick paste.

6 Dip the prepared vegetables into the thick paste and deep-fry them.

Deep-Fried Kelp
Tashimat'wigim (다시마튀김)

1 Wrap the kelp in a damp cloth.

3 Remove the tops from the pine nuts.

5 Cut both edges into a deep-V like a ribbon.

2 Cut the kelp into ⅓" × 4" pieces.

4 Slip the pine nut into the knot.

6 Deep-fry the kelp until crisp in oil at 340°F and sprinkle with sugar.

Ingredients   1 piece kelp, ¼ cup pine nuts, sugar, oil

Method   **1** Wrap the kelp in a damp cloth.
2 When the kelp gets moist, cut it into ⅓" × 4" pieces.
3 Remove the tops from the pine nuts.
4 Tie the kelp like a ribbon and place the pine nut in the center.
5 Cut both edges neatly with a scissors.

6 Heat the oil to 340°F and deep-fry the ribbon-shaped kelp until crisp. Drain and sprinkle with the sugar.
7 Arrange the deep-fried kelp attractively on paper in a basket.

Hint   Deep-fry the kelp on medium heat in oil until crisp. This is a tasty dried side dish with wine.

Oysters Fried in Egg Batter
Kuljŏn (굴전)

1 Clean the oysters in salt water and drain.

3 Dip the #2 oysters into flour.

2 Sprinkle the clean oysters with the ginger juice and black pepper and mix well.

4 Dip the #3 oysters into beaten egg and fry in an oiled pan.

Ingredients ⅔ lb. oysters, ½ cup flour, 2 eggs, 10 gingko nuts, ginger juice, salt, black pepper, parsley, MSG

Method 1 Buy fresh, large oysters. Wash them in salt water, remove the shells and drain.

2 Sprinkle the clean oysters with the black pepper and ginger juice.

3 Dip the oysters into flour and then into the beaten egg. Fry them in a hot oiled pan.

4 Stir-fry the shelled gingko nuts with salt and peel off the skin.

5 Arrange the fried oysters in a dish and garnish with the ginko nuts and parsley.

Fried Stuffed Pepper
P'utkoch'ujŏn (풋고추전)

Ingredients   10 small, long Korean green peppers, 2 red peppers, 2 green bell peppers, ⅓ lb. beef, ⅓ cake bean curd, ½ tsp. soy sauce, 1 tsp. salt, 1 green onion, 4 cloves garlic, 1 tbsp. sesame salt, ¼ tsp. black pepper, 2 tsp. sesame oil, 2 eggs, flour

Method   **1** Halve the small green and red peppers. Cut the bell peppers into ¼″ thick rings. Remove the seeds.
2 Soak the **#1** peppers in salt water and then pat dry. Dip the insides of the pepper halves lightly into flour.
3 Mix the minced beef and mashed bean curd with the seasoning.
4 Stuff the pepper halves and bell pepper rings with the beef mixture.
5 Dip the stuffed side of the pepper into flour and then into beaten egg and fry in a pan until the meat gets cooked through. Dip both sides of the stuffed bell pepper into flour, then into beaten egg and fry until golden brown.

Hint   The green pepper contains good amounts of vitamin A. The hot taste of the pepper quickens the secretion of gastric juice and the circulation of the blood.

1 Halve the peppers, slice the bell peppers and remove the seeds.

2 Soak the **#1** peppers in salt water and drain.

3 Mix the beef and bean curd with the seasoning.

4 Dip the inside of the peppers into flour. Stuff them with the **#3** mixture and dip them into flour again.

5 Dip the stuffed peppers into beaten egg and fry until golden brown.

53

Mung Bean Pancake
Pindaettŏk (빈대떡)

Ingredients 1 cup dried mung beans, ⅓ cup rice, ½ cup water, 1 oz. pork, ginger, 1 clove garlic, sesame oil, MSG, 1 oz. kimchi, red pepper thread, 2 green onions, cherry, parsley

Method **1** Soak the mung beans several hours in water and rub off the skins. Grind soaked rice and the mung beans with water in a blender.

2 Cut the pork into thin strips and mix it with the chopped garlic, ginger and seasoning.

3 Squeeze the water from the kimchi. Cut it into thin strips and mix it with sesame oil.

4 Drop the **#1** batter by table-spoonfuls onto a hot oiled pan and top it evenly with the vegetable and pork strips. Fry until golden brown.

Hint It tastes better to fry the batter in pork fat instead of oil.

1 Grind the soaked rice and mung beans with water in a blender.

3 Cut the pork into thin strips and season.

2 Squeeze the water from the kimchi. Cut it into thin strips and mix it with sesame oil.

4 Drop the batter onto a greased pan and top with the kimchi, pork, green onion and red pepper thread.

Fried Green Onion
P'ajŏn (파전)

Ingredients ¼ lb. small green onion, ¼ bundle watercress, 1 oz. pork, ½ cup sea mussel, ½ cup rice powder, 1 egg, salt, vinegar-soy sauce, lettuce

Method 1 Trim the small green onions and watercress and cut them into 4" lengths.

2 Slice the pork thinly and chop the sea mussel finely.

3 Add a little water to the rice flour and a little salt and mix into a light batter.

4 Spread the sliced green onions in an oiled pan and place the sliced watercress between the green onion slices.

5 Arrange the pork and sea mussel evenly on the #4 vegetables. Spread the #3 batter on the top and cook slightly. Then cover the top with beaten egg and fry until golden brown. Serve with vinegar-soy sauce for dipping.

1 Cut the small green onions and watercress into 4" lengths.

2 Chop the sea mussel and slice the pork thinly.

3 Mix the rice flour, salt and a little water into a light batter.

4 Place the #1, #2 ingredients in an oiled pan and spread the #3 batter on the top.

5 When the #4 patty gets cooked slightly, cover it with beaten egg and fry.

Fried Zucchini
Hobakchŏn (호박전)

1 Cut the young zucchini into ¼" thick circles.

4 Dry the squash slices and dip them into flour and top them with the **#3** mixture evenly.

5 Cover the zucchini slices with beaten egg and fry until golden brown.

2 Sprinkle the squash slices with the salt.

3 Mix the minced beef and mashed bean curd with the seasoning.

Ingredients 1 zucchini, 2 oz. beef, 1 egg, ½ cake bean curd, 1 green onion, 1 clove garlic, ¼ cup flour, 4 tbsp. salt, 1 red pepper

Method **1** Cut the zucchini into ¼" thick circles and sprinkle it with the salt.
2 Mince the beef finely.
3 Mix the mashed bean curd, minced beef and beaten egg with the seasoning.
4 Dry the squash slices and dip them into flour. Spoon the **#3** mixture on the center of the squash slice. Then dip them into flour and into beaten egg and fry until golden brown.
5 Decorate with the red pepper and serve with the seasoning sauce.

Fried Zucchini

Skewered Garlic
Manǔl Sanjŏk (마늘 산적)

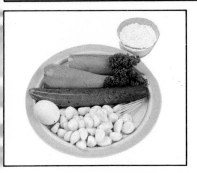

Ingredients   40 cloves garlic, 2 oz. ham, 1 carrot, 1 cucumber, 2 tbsp. soy sauce, sesame oil, MSG, 2 eggs, ½ cup flour, parsley, skewers

Method   **1** Scald the garlic slightly in hot salt water.

2 Cut the ham, cucumber and carrot into the same size as the garlic and season them with the soy sauce, sesame oil and MSG.

3 On skewers, string the garlic, ham, cucumber and carrot slices in order and dip the under side of the skewered food into flour.

4 Dip the skewered food into beaten egg and fry in a greased pan.

1 Scald the garlic briefly in salt water.

2 Cut the ham, cucumber and carrot into the same size as the garlic.

3 Season the **#1, #2** ingredients with the soy sauce, sesame oil and MSG.

4 Dip the under side of the skewered food into flour and dip them into beaten egg and fry.

Skewered Garlic

Skewered Fish
Ŏsanjŏk (어산적)

1 Mince the beef finely and season.

3 Season the fish pieces with the salt, sesame oil and MSG.

5 Fill the space with the seasoned beef.

2 Slice thinly and then cut the butterfish into 2¾" lengths.

4 Skewer #3 leaving space between each one to stuff with the beef.

6 Pound the skewered food with the back of a knife gently and fry.

Ingredients   **A**   ¼ lb. beef, ½ tbsp. soy sauce, 1 tsp. sugar, 1 tsp. sesame oil, sesame salt, black pepper, green onion, garlic
B   2 butterfish, ½ tbsp. salt, 1 tsp. sesame oil, MSG
C   1 bundle parsley, 6 cherries, pine nut powder

Method   **1** Mince the beef finely and season it with the **A** ingredients.
2 Remove the head, tail and entrails from the butterfish and skin it. Slice thinly and cut the fish into ¼" thick and 2¾" long rectangles.
3 Season the fish pieces with the salt, sesame oil and MSG. Skewer the fish pieces leaving space between each one to be filled with the meat.
4 Fill the space with the seasoned beef, pound the skewered food with the back of a knife to tenderize and fry in a fry pan.
5 Serve the fried skewered food garnished with parsley and cherry on a plate.

58

Vegetable Salads
Cold Vegetable Dishes
Raw Salads

Mung Bean Sprout Salad
Sukchunamul (숙주나물)

Bracken Salad
Kosarinamul (고사리나물)

Ingredients   ½ lb. mung bean sprouts, 1 tbsp. soy sauce, 1 tbsp. chopped garlic, 1 tbsp. sesame salt, 2 tsp. salt, 2 tsp. sesame oil, sesame seed, MSG, red pepper thread

Method   **1** Clean the mung bean sprouts, scald them in boiling salted water and drain.

2 Sprinkle the seasoning sauce on the scalded mung bean sprouts and mix well. Top them with the red pepper threads and sesame seed and serve.

1 Scald the mung bean sprouts in boiling salted water.

2 Mix the seasoning to make the seasoning sauce.

3 Sprinkle the seasoning sauce on the scalded mung bean sprouts and mix well.

Ingredients   ½ lb. bracken, salt, 1 tsp. soy sauce, 1 tsp. sugar, 1 tbsp. chopped garlic, 1 tbsp. sesame oil, 1 tbsp. sesame salt, 2 tbsp. oil, MSG

Method   **1** Soak the bracken in water and remove the tough stems. Cut into 4" lengths and squeeze out the water.

2 Stir-fry the bracken in an oiled pan sprinkling it with the sesame salt, chopped garlic, sesame oil, MSG, salt and soy sauce.

1 Soak the bracken in water and remove the tough stems. Cut it into 4" lengths.

2 Stir-fry the bracken in an oiled pan.

3 Season to taste.

Mung Bean Sprout Salad

Seasoned Dried Pollack
Pugŏmuch'im (북어무침)

Ingredients **A** 1 dried pollack
B 1 tsp. sugar, 1 tsp. salt, ½ tsp.
sesame oil, 1 tsp. sesame salt
C 1 tsp. sugar, 1 tsp. salt, ½ tsp.
sesame oil, 1 tsp. sesame salt, 1 tsp.
red pepper powder, 3 tbsp. salad oil
D 1 tsp. sugar, 1 tsp. sesame salt,
½ tsp. sesame oil

Method **1** Pound the dried
pollack with a wooden mallet and
peel. Remove the dried flesh from

Bracken Salad

the bones and head.
2 Shred the flesh finely and wrap
it in a damp cloth to soften.
3 Pound the wrapped flesh in a
mortar to fluff it up.
4 Rub the **#3** flesh with your
hands to soften.
5 Divide the shredded flesh into
three equal parts. Mix the **B**, **C**
and **D** ingredients separately with
one-third the flesh to make three

colors. When mixing the **C** ingredients add some red pepper oil.

Hint Buy yellow dried pollack.
You may pound the dried pollack
with a mallet or use the dried pollack slices.

1 Pound the dried pollack with a
mallet.

3 Rub the **#2** flesh with your hands
to fluff it up.

2 Shred the flesh finely and wrap it in
a damp cloth. Pound the wrapped
flesh with a mallet in a mortar.

4 Mix the flesh (divided into three
equal parts) separately with the three
seasonings— **B**, **C**, **D**.

Garland Chrysanthemum Salad   Jellied Mung-Bean Puree
Ssukkatmuch'im (쑥갓무침)   **Ch'ongp'omuch'im** (청포무침)

Ingredients   1 bundle garland chrysanthemum, ½ tbsp. soy sauce, ½ tbsp. salt, green onion, garlic, sesame oil, sesame salt

Method   1 Trim the garland chrysanthemum and remove any tough stems.

2 Scald the garland chrysanthemum in boiling salted water. Rinse it in cold water and drain.

3 Squeeze the water from the scalded garland chrysanthemum and season it with the chopped green onion and garlic.

1 Scald the garland chrysanthemum (starting with the stems) in boiling salted water and rinse it in cold water.

2 Season with the soy sauce, sesame salt, garlic, green onion, red pepper thread and sesame oil.

Jellied Mung-Bean Puree

Ingredients   2 cakes jellied mung-bean, ½ carrot, 1 cucumber, 2 oz. kimchi, 4 oz. soy bean sprouts, 1 egg, 1 oz. green bell pepper, ½ tsp. soy sauce, 1 tsp. salt, 1 tbsp. vinegar, 1 tbsp. sugar, ½ tbsp. sesame salt, sesame oil

Method   1 Cut the jellied mung-bean puree into ¼" thick strips and mix it with the sesame oil and salt. Squeeze the water from the kimchi and cut it into thin strips. Mix it with the sesame oil and sugar.

2 Cut the beef into thin strips and season it with the green onion, garlic, soy sauce, sugar, sesame salt and black pepper. Fry and cool it. Cut the carrot into thin strips and fry it with salt slightly.

3 Remove the hairlike roots from the bean sprouts. Scald the sprouts

Todok Salad
Tŏdŏkmuch'im (더덕무침)

Ingredients   ¼ lb. todok (a white root), ½ bundle watercress, 1 tbsp. red pepper paste, 1 tbsp. vinegar, 1 tbsp. sugar, green onion, garlic, sesame oil, sesame salt, lettuce

Method   **1** Pound the todok with a mallet and wash by rubbing it with your hands in salt water. Shred it finely and squeeze out the water.
2 Cut the watercress into 2" lengths.
3 Mix the todok and watercress with the vinegar-red pepper paste. Serve the todok salad on lettuce leaves.

Hint   Todok loses its puckery taste if rubbed in salt water. Todok salad, seasoned with vinegar and sugar, will stimulate your appetite. Todok is a low calorie food.

1 Soak the todok in salt water and drain.

2 Shred the todok finely.

3 Mix the todok and watercress with the vinegar-red pepper paste.

in salted water, drain and mix them with the sesame oil.
4 Remove the seeds from the bell pepper and red pepper and cut them into thin strips.
5 Cut the cucumber into thin strips and sprinkle it with salt. Squeeze out the water and fry lightly. Fry the beaten egg into a thin sheet and cut it into thin strips.
6 Mix all the ingredients with the vinegar-soy sauce. Sprinkle with the powdered laver and serve.

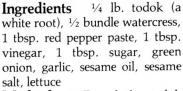

1 Cut the jellied mung-bean puree into thick strips and mix it with the sesame oil and salt.

3 Cut the carrot into thin strips, fry it lightly and salt it.

2 Remove the hairlike roots from the bean sprouts. Scald them and mix with the sesame oil.

4 Mix the jellied mung-bean puree, bean sprouts, cucumber and carrot strips with the vinegar-soy sauce.

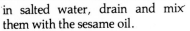

Seasoned Cucumber with Vinegar Ginseng Rootlet Salad
Oich'omuch'im (오이초무침) **Misammuch'im** (미삼무침)

1 Soak the cucumber and radish slices in the vinegar-water.

2 Drain and mix the marinated vegetables with the lemon pieces.

3 Sprinkle with the sesame seed and red pepper thread.

Ginseng Rootlet Salad

1 Clean and drain the rootlets of ginseng.

Ingredients   ½ lb. rootlets of ginseng, salt, 1 tbsp. soy sauce, 2 tsp. sugar, green onion, garlic, ½ tbsp. sesame salt, 1 tsp. sesame oil
Method   **1** Wash the rootlets of ginseng until clean and drain.
2 Steam the rootlets of ginseng on a damp cloth in a steamer and place them in a wicker tray.
3 Mix the chopped green onion and garlic with the seasonings to make the sauce.
4 Mix the steamed rootlets with the seasoning sauce.
Hint   Even if you mix the root-

Ingredients 2 cucumbers, ¼ white Korean radish, ½ lemon, vinegar, 2 tbsp. sugar, 1 tbsp. salt, 1 tsp. sesame seed, red pepper thread

Method 1 Clean the cucumbers by rubbing them with salt and drain. Cut them into slices 2" long. Sprinkle with salt and allow them to stand. Squeeze out the water.

2 Cut the radish into the same size as the cucumber slices.

3 Cut the lemon into ginko leaf-shaped pieces.

4 Combine the salt, vinegar and sugar to make the sauce. Sprinkle the cucumber and radish slices with the sauce and let them stand.

5 Mix the lemon and marinated vegetable slices.

6 Sprinkle the sesame seed and red pepper thread on the mixture and serve with the seasoning sauce; 2 tbsp. vinegar, 1 tbsp. sugar and 1 tsp. soy sauce.

Hint Place the cucumber in a dry cloth and squeeze out the water by pressing it down gently.

2 Steam the rootlets of ginseng in a steamer.

3 Mix the steamed rootlets with the seasoning sauce.

lets of ginseng with a vinegar-red pepper paste, the fragrance of ginseng will prevail and stimulate your appetite.

Ingredients ⅓ lb. fresh brown seaweed, ¼ lb. crab meat jelly, ½ cucumber, 1 tbsp. vinegar, 1 tbsp. red pepper powder, 1 clove garlic, 2 tsp. salt, 1 tbsp. sugar, ½ tsp. sesame salt

Method 1 Clean the fresh seaweed and scald it in boiling water for 3 minutes. Rinse it in cold water and cut it into small pieces.

1 Clean the fresh seaweed and scald it in boiling water for 3 minutes.

2 Rinse the scalded seaweed in cold water and cut it into small pieces.

2 Halve the cucumber and cut it into half-circles. Sprinkle them with the salt and squeeze out the water.

3 Shred the crab meat jelly.

4 Mix the seaweed, cucumber pieces and crab meat jelly with the red pepper powder, garlic, sesame salt, vinegar and sugar.

Hint You may cook the fresh seaweed as it is without scalding.

3 Shred the crab meat jelly.

4 Mix the seaweed, crab meat jelly and cucumber pieces with the seasoning.

Bellflower Root Salad
Toraji Saengch'ae (도라지 생채)

White Radish Salad
Muu Saengch'ae (무우 생채)

Ingredients ½ lb. bellflower roots, ½ cucumber, 2 tbsp. red pepper powder, 2 cloves garlic, 1 tbsp. chopped green onion, 1½ tbsp. sugar, 1 tsp. salt, ½ tsp. soy sauce, 1 tbsp. vinegar

Method **1** Shred the bellflower roots finely using a toothpick.

2 Clean the shredded bellflower by rubbing it with the salt. Squeeze out the water.

3 Cut the cucumber into half-circles. Sprinkle with salt and squeeze out the water.

4 Mix the bellflower roots and cucumber pieces with the seasoning and vinegar.

Hint Rub the bellflower roots with salt to remove the bitterness. Squeeze the cucumber tightly.

1 Shred the bellflower roots using a toothpick.

2 Rub the shredded bellflower with salt.

3 Squeeze out the water and season.

Ingredients ½ lb. white Korean radish, ½ tbsp. red pepper powder, 1 tsp. salt, 1 tbsp. sugar, 1 green onion, 1 clove garlic, vinegar, lettuce

Method **1** Peel the radish and cut it into 2″ long, thin strips.

2 Mix the radish strips with the red pepper powder.

3 Add the sugar, salt, red pepper threads, green onion and chopped garlic to the **#2** mixture.

4 Sprinkle the **#3** mixture with the vinegar and mix well.

Hint Sprinkle the radish with salt and squeeze out the water, then season it once again to taste.

White Radish Salad

Cold Cooked Jellyfish
Haep'ari Naengch'ae (해파리 냉채)

1 Cut the carrot, cucumber, egg sheets and jellyfish into thin strips.

2 Mix the radish strips with the red pepper powder first.

3 Make the garlic sauce.

Ingredients   **A** ⅔ lb. jellyfish, 1 cucumber, ½ carrot, 1 egg
B 3 cloves garlic, ¼ cup water, 1 tbsp. vinegar, ½ tsp. salt, 1 tsp. sugar, ½ tsp. soy sauce, ½ tsp. sesame oil
C 3½ tbsp. dry mustard, 1½ tbsp. sugar, 1 tbsp. salt, ½ tbsp. soy sauce, ¼ cup vinegar, ¼ cup water

Method   **1** Buy tender jellyfish and soak it in cold water to remove the salt water, then scald it in water at 140°F.
2 Cut the scalded jellyfish into thin strips and marinate it in the sugar and vinegar.
3 Cut the cucumber and carrot into thin strips.

4 Fry the beaten egg yolk and white separately into thin sheets and cut them into thin strips.
5 Mix the chopped garlic with the **B** ingredients to make the garlic sauce.
6 Mix the mustard with the **C** ingredients to make the mustard sauce.
7 Mix the **#2** jellyfish and cucumber strips. Place the mixture in the center of a plate and surround it with alternating spokes of the egg, carrot and cucumber strips.
8 Serve with the garlic sauce and the mustard sauce.
Hint   If you scald the jellyfish in water hotter than 160°F it becomes tough.

1 Cut the radish into 2″ long, thin strips.

2 Mix the **#1** ingredients with the vinegar and sugar.

3 Add the remaining seasonings and mix well.

Mustard Salad
Kyŏjach'ae (겨자채)

1 Place the bowl containing the mustard paste face down on a hot pot and let it stand.

2 Cut the ham into thin strips.

3 Cut the cucumber, carrot and egg sheet into thin strips.

4 Score the squid diagonally and cut it into thin strips.

5 Grind the pine nuts in a mortar adding the mustard-vinegar sauce.

Ingredients ¼ lb. ham, 1 cucumber, ¼ pear, ½ carrot, 1 squid, ¼ lb. jellyfish, 5 chestnuts, 1 egg, 7 tbsp. dry mustard, 3 tbsp. pine nuts, 1 tbsp. soy sauce, 3 tbsp. sugar, 2 tbsp. salt, ½ cup vinegar, ½ cup water

Method **1** Cut the ham into thin strips.

2 Cut the cucumber, carrot and egg sheets into the same strips as the ham.

3 Peel and cut the pear into thin strips. Soak it in sugar water.

4 Slice the chestnuts thinly.

5 Halve the squid. Score it crosswise and lengthwise at ¼″ intervals and cut it into thin strips. Scald and cool.

6 Rinse the jellyfish three times to remove the salt water and scald it in water at 140°F. Cut it into thin strips and mix it with the vinegar and sugar.

7 Slowly stir boiling water into the mustard; stir until a smooth paste forms in the bowl. Put the bowl containing the mustard paste face down on a hot pot and let it stand for 10-15 minutes. When the mustard is complete, add the soy sauce, sugar, vinegar, water and salt and mix well. Grind the pine nuts in a mortar adding the above mustard mixture to make the mustard-vinegar sauce.

8 Arrange the prepared vegetables attractively around the mustard-vinegar sauce.

Hint **1** After removing the tops from the pine nuts, grind the pine nuts in a mortar, so that they do not float on top of the mustard-vinegar sauce.

2 You may use boiled beef, pork or chicken instead of the ham.

5-Color Bean Sprout Dish

K'ongnamul Osaekch'ae (콩나물 오색채)

Ingredients   ½ bundle water-cress, ½ cup water, ½ carrot, 1½ tsp. salt, ½ lb. bean sprouts, 1 egg, 2 oz. beef, 3 dried brown, oak mushrooms, ½ round onion, 1 tsp. sesame oil, 1 green onion, black pepper, MSG

Method   **1** Place the trimmed bean sprouts (without the hairlike roots) with ½ cup water and 1 tsp. salt in a covered pan and bring to a boil. When cooked, mix them with the sesame oil.

2 Cut the carrot into thin strips and stir-fry with salt.
3 Cut the watercress into 2" lengths and stir-fry with salt.
4 Fry the beaten egg into a sheet and cut it into thin strips.
5 Cut the beef, dried mushrooms and round onion into thin strips, season and fry.
6 Arrange the bean sprouts, carrot, watercress and egg strips in circles around the beef-mushroom mixture in the center of the plate.

1 Boil the bean sprouts with the salt and water.

3 Cut the egg sheet, carrot and water-cress into thin strips.

2 Mix the boiled bean sprouts with the sesame oil.

4 Fry the beef, dried mushroom and round onion strips.

Sliced Raw Skate
Hongŏhoe (홍어회)

Ingredients   1 skate, ½ Korean hard pear, ½ white Korean radish, ½ bundle watercress, 2 green peppers, pine nuts, lettuce, 4 tbsp. red pepper paste, 7 tbsp. vinegar, 1 tbsp. sugar, 1 tbsp. sesame salt, 1 tsp. sesame oil, 1 green onion, 4 cloves garlic, MSG, 1 tbsp. red pepper powder, 2 red peppers

Method   **1** Skin and cut the skate diagonally into bite-sized pieces. Sprinkle with 4 tbsp. vinegar and let them stand. Then squeeze out the water.

2 Cut the radish and pear into the same size as the skate pieces. Sprinkle the radish with the salt, vinegar and sugar and squeeze out the water. Soak the pear in sugar water and drain.

3 Cut the watercress, red peppers and green peppers into the same size as the skate pieces.

4 Combine the **#1**, **#2** and **#3** ingredients well with the seasonings.

5 Place the **#4** mixture on lettuce leaves on a plate and sprinkle the top with the pine nuts.

Ingredients   ½ lb. tuna, 1 butterfish, 2 abalones, 1 squid, 1 laver, 5 blood clams, ¼ cucumber, 3 cherries, 2 lettuce leaves, 1 piece turnip, 1 piece carrot, 1 tbsp. lemon juice, 2 tbsp. red pepper paste, 1 clove garlic, 1 green onion, 1 tsp. sesame salt, 1 tsp. sesame oil

Method   **1** Slice the tuna thinly and cut it into bite-sized pieces.

2 Skin the butterfish and remove the entrails. Slice the flesh into bite-sized pieces.

3 Clean the abalones by rubbing them with salt and removing the entrails and shells. Slice the abalone flesh thinly and place the slices in the shells.

4 Remove the entrails, head and

1 Sprinkle the sliced skate with the vinegar and squeeze out the water.

3 Sprinkle the radish pieces with the vinegar, sugar and salt and squeeze out the water.

1 Slice the tuna thinly and cut it into bite-sized pieces.

2 Cut the pear and radish into the same size as the skate pieces. Soak the pear pieces in sugar water and drain.

4 Combine the #1, #2 and #3 ingredients thoroughly with the seasoned red pepper paste.

Raw Fish Variety Plate
Modŭmhoe (모듬회)

Green Onion Bundles
Shilp'aganghoe (실파강회)

legs from the squid and skin it. Score the body of the squid at ¼″ intervals.

5 Spread the sheet of laver on the inside of the squid, roll it up and wrap it firmly. Cut the roll into bite-sized rings.

6 Remove the flesh from the shells of the blood clams. Clean it and cut it into bite-sized pieces.

7 Arrange the prepared ingredients on a layer of shredded white radish and garnish with the cucumber, cherries and flower-shaped carrots.

8 Serve with the vinegar-red pepper paste.

2 Slice the flesh of abalone thinly and place it in the shell.

3 Skin and score the squid.

4 Place the sheet of laver on the body of the squid, roll it up and cut it into slices.

Ingredients 1 bundle small green onion, 2 eggs, ½ lb. ham, 2 tbsp. pine nut, red pepper thread, 1 tbsp. red pepper paste, 1 tbsp. sugar, 1 tsp. chopped green onion, 1 tsp. chopped garlic, 1 tbsp. vinegar, pine nut powder

Method **1** Scald the small green onions (starting with the stems) in salted water.

2 Fry the beaten egg yolk and white separately into thick sheets and cut them into pieces ⅓″ × 1⅔″. Cut the ham into the same size as the egg.

4 Arrange the egg white, ham and yolk in order and place red pepper threads and pine nuts on the top. Then tie them with the small green onion to make a bundle.

5 Serve the **#4** bundles with the vinegar-red pepper paste sauce sprinkled with powdered pine nuts for dipping.

Green Onion Bundles

Watercress Bundles
Minariganghoe (미나리강회)

1 Scald the watercress stems in boiling salted water and rinse them in cold water.

2 Skin the squid and score it diagonally. Cut into thick strips and scald it in boiling salted water.

3 Tie the squid strips with the scalded watercress stems to make a bundle.

Ingredients   2 bundles watercress, 1 squid, 2 tbsp. red pepper paste, 1 tbsp. vinegar, 1 tbsp. sugar, 1 tbsp. powdered pine nuts

Method   **1** Remove the leaves from the watercress and clean. Parboil the stems in boiling salted water and rinse them in cold water.

2 Skin the body of the squid and score it diagonally

at ¼" intervals. Cut into thick strips and scald it in boiling salted water. Mix the seasonings to make the seasoned red pepper paste.

3 Place the red pepper thread on the squid strips and tie them with the scalded watercress to make a bundle. Serve the bundles with the seasoned red pepper paste for dipping.

1 Scald the small green onions (starting with the stems) in salted water.

2 Cut the ham and egg sheets into pieces ⅓" × 1⅔"

3 Arrange #2, red pepper thread and pine nut in order. Then tie them with the small green onion to make a bundle.

72

GLOSSARY

Angelica Shoots (turŭp) are young shoots with tender green leaves of the angelica bush which are available fresh only in early spring.

Bamboo Shoots (chuksun) are the tender spring sprouts of the bamboo, off-white in color and shaped like a bud. Their flesh is tender but firm and should be scalded about 5 minutes in boiling water if used fresh.

Barley Tea (porich'a) is tea made from toasted barley kernels. It is prepared by adding the toasted barley to boiling water, boiling for 5 minutes, straining and serving. Barley tea is served cooled in the summer and warm in the winter. Corn tea is prepared and served the same way but is made from parched corn kernels.

Bean Curd (tubu) is a square or rectangular cake of pressed, coagulated soybean puree—the "cheese" of soymilk. It has a bland texture and is a very easy-to-digest, nutritious food. It should be kept in water (changing water daily) in the refrigerator.

Beans: There are a large variety of dried beans available in the Korean grain-bean shops. In addition there are various processed bean foods also available for daily use in the Korean diet.

— yellow soybeans (hŭink'ong), sprouts (k'ongnamul), bean curd (tubu), soft bean curd (sundubu), bean paste (toenjang), fermented soybeans for making soy sauce (meju), seasoned fermented soybeans (ch'ŏnggukchang), soybean flour (k'ongkaru), soy sauce (kanjang).

— Brown soybeans (pamk'ong—literally "chestnut beans") are a chestnut brown color and have a smooth chestnut-like texture when cooked.

— Black soybeans (kŏmŭnk'ong) are served as a side dish.

— mung beans (noktu), sprouts (sukchu namul), jellied mung bean puree (ch'ŏngp'o), mung bean flour (noktu karu).

— red kidney beans (kangnamk'ong)

Bean Sprouts (k'ongnamul) may be grown at home, if desired, in a warm, wet jar or purchased in most vegetable sections of grocery stores. The large sprouts are from the yellow soybean; the smaller more delicate sprouts are from the green mung bean.

Bellflower Root (toraji) is a white root from the mountainside bellflower.

Bracken (kosari) is the early spring shoot of the fern plant. These shoots are gathered in the spring and sold fresh at that time. They are also dried for re-hydration later in the year. There is a common variety and a rather special royal fern variety that has larger, softer shoots.

Burdock Root (uŏng) is a long, fat nutritious root with a distinctive flavor which is washed, scrubbed and scraped, soaked in vinegar-water so that it does not change color and then cut into thick strips for use.

Chinese Cabbage (paech'u) is a solid, oblong head of wide stalk-leaves with a subtle flavor used widely in making kimchi.

Chinese Noodles (tangmyŏn) are very thin transparent noodles made from mung bean flour. They are sold dried in long loops. They should be soaked in warm water before use and cooked quickly. When cooked they become opaque and slippery.

Cinnamon (kyep'i) is a rough brown bark. It can be used whole or dried and ground to use in seasoning.

Eggplant (kaji) is the long, purple, shiny fruit of the eggplant plant; it is not large and round but sleek and elongated with a slight bulbousness at the end opposite the stem.

Garland Chrysanthemum (ssukkat) is a pungent, edible variety of Chrysanthemum; the leaves are used for seasoning and decorating like lettuce leaves in Korean recipes.

Garlic (manŭl), related to the onion, has a bulb made up of several cloves with a strong odor and flavor. It is widely used as seasoning in Korean dishes after being finely chopped. Garlic is also served pickled and its long green stems are eaten raw or boiled.

Ginger Root (saenggang) adds zip to many Korean dishes. Fresh ginger root has a thin light-brown skin over knobby bulbs. It may be washed and dried and placed in the freezer in a plastic bag. It is then available for grating into whatever dish is being prepared. It may be dried and powdered but fresh ginger is called for in most Korean recipes.

Gingko Nuts (ŭnhaeng) are oval-shaped, yellowish nuts with a soft texture. The shelled nuts may be stir-fried until green after which the outer skin will peel off easily. The peeled nuts are used for garnish on many special Korean dishes.

Ginseng (insam) is a much-prized root cultivated in Korea and China. This perennial herb is used mostly for medicinal purposes and is widely acclaimed for its rejuvenating qualities. It is usually sold dried, but fresh roots and rootlets are used in cooking. Ginseng tea and wine are popular in Korea.

Glutinous Rice (ch'apssal) is a white rice with a sticky consistency when cooked.

Glutinous Rice Flour (ch'apssal karu) is the flour from glutinous rice which is used in making Korean rice cakes.

Grain Syrup(choch'ŏng) is similar to dark corn syrup and is used as a sweetener. It is made by boiling "yot," a Korean candy base, with water and sugar until thick. Honey or sugar syrup can be used instead of this grain syrup in most recipes.

Green Onions: There are many varieties of green onions in Korea.

— (ch'ŏngp'a)—a medium sized variety harvested in the spring

— (puch'u)—a small, wild leek with a pungent flavor

— (shilp'a)—a thread-like onion with a taste similar to but stronger than chives

— (tallae)—a small, wild onion from the mountain meadows

Green Peppers, Korean (p'utkoch'u), are long, narrow unripe chili peppers and are usually hot to taste.

Indian Mustard Leaf (kat) is a green leaf available spring and autumn; Japanese "haruna."

Jujubes (taech'u) are similar to a date, usually used dried, for cooking or medicinal purposes. They should be soaked before using.

Kimchi is a spicy, slightly fermented pickle like vegetable dish accompanying every Korean meal. It is made from Chinese cabbage, Korean white radish, cucumber or other seasonal vegetables which are wilted with salt, stuffed with seasoning such as red pepper powder, chopped garlic, ginger juice and soused salted shrimp juice and fermented in earthenware crocks.

Konyak is jellied potato puree; it is sliced and used somewhat like a noodle.

Laver (kim) is cultivated carefully in the seabeds offshore in Korea and is of excellent quality. It is sold in packages of folded paper-thin sheets. It is used for wrapping rice rolls or broiled to a delicate crispness and served with a rice meal.

Lotus Root (yŏn-gūn) is the root of the lotus flower. It is grey on the outside but when cut open a beautiful lacy effect is formed in each slice by several open tubes which run the length of the root. It is served as a vegetable or candied as a sweet.

Malt Powder (yŏtkirūm) is dried sprouted barley which has been crushed into a powder. It is used to aid fermentation in making wines and drinks; it is a good food for yeast.

Mushrooms: There are several varieties used both fresh and dried.

— Brown oak mushrooms (p'yogo) (Japanese shiitake) are used in meat dishes after soaking well in warm water.

— Stone mushrooms (sōgi) also should be soaked before using.

— Jew's ear mushrooms (mogi) are large, delicate ear-shaped fungi.

— Pine mushrooms (songi) grow on pine tree trunks; they are most often sold fresh or canned; very tasty when sliced and sauteed.

Pear, Korean (pae) is a crisp, large, round, firm, sweet, apple-like pear which is very juicy. It has a tan outside skin and a cream-colored flesh with dark brown seeds. Harvested in the fall it keeps well in rice-hulls in a cool place. It is considered to be an aid in digestion.

Pine Nut (chat) is the nut-like edible, soft-textured, somewhat oily seeds of the pinon tree. They are used to make a gruel-soup and in garnishing drinks and other foods.

Pine Nut Powder is ground or finely chopped pine nuts used for rolling sweet rice cakes and other delicacies.

Pulgogi is Korea's best-known charcoal-broiled marinated beef dish. It is traditionally broiled over charcoal in a slotted pan but it may be oven-broiled or quickly pan-broiled.

Radish, Korean White (muu) is a round, long, firm white root much larger than a red or white table radish. The taste is sweet when first harvested and its texture is crisp and juicy. It is a basic kimchi ingredient; it is sometimes dried for making soups in the winter and small, young radishes are used for a special spring kimchi.

Red Pepper Paste (koch'ujang) is a dark reddish paste made from fermented soybean and red pepper powder mixed with glutinous rice flour and malt. It is spicy hot and widely used to thicken and season soups and stews. It will keep well in the refrigerator.

Red Peppers (koch'u) are a basic Korean seasoning ingredient. They are small, long peppers similar to cayenne and are hot to the taste. They are dried and ground or cut into threads or used fresh for seasoning or garnish. They are very high in vitamin A.

Rice Cake (ttŏk) is a delicacy served at most celebrations in Korea. It is made by steaming a glutinous rice flour dough which has been filled or mixed with various foods such as sesame seed, beans, mugwort, nuts, jujube, raisins; the dough is usually shaped beautifully into half-moons, circles or other soft shapes.

Rice Wine (ch'ŏngju) is a clear white wine made from rice used for drinking and cooking.

Salted Soused Shrimp (saeujŏt) are tiny shrimp which have been salted and become somewhat pickled and juicy; used in making kimchi and in seasoning.

Sesame Leaves (kkaennip) are the beautifully shaped pungent leaves of the sesame plant which are served as a vegetable in a sauce or deep-batter-fried.

Sesame Oil (ch'amgirūm) is pressed from toasted sesame seeds. It has a unique flavor and only a little is needed to add an authentic taste to Korean dishes.

Sesame Salt (kkaesogūm) is a mixture of toasted, crushed sesame seeds and salt. Add 1 teaspoon of salt to each cup of seeds. It is a basic Korean seasoning.

Sesame Seeds: White (hŭinkkae), black (kŏmŭnkkae) and round brown (tŭlkkae) are all used in Korean seasoning and in Korean candy-cookies.

Shinsollo is the name of a one-dish meal which is cooked at the table in a brass brazier "hot pot" which holds the charcoal in the center allowing the food to cook around it in a well-seasoned broth. It is a special occasion dish requiring hours of preserving preparation so that each food is cut precisely to the right shape and partially pre-cooked to allow for just the right last minute cooking at the table.

Soybean Paste (toenjang) is a thick brown paste made from a mixture of mashed fermented soybean lumps (left from making the soy sauce), powdered red pepper seeds and salt. It is used as a thickener for soups and stews and will keep well in the refrigerator.

Soy Sauce (kanjang) is a brownish-black salty liquid made by cooking fermented soybean cakes with water and salt. Each household in Korea used to make their own soy sauce in the spring; some still do. These are mild and add good flavor to most any food. Soy sauce is used in cooking, especially meats, but is also placed on the table to use as a dip for sauteed vegetables, fish and meat. The Japanese soy sauce is less salty but sweeter than Korean soy sauce.

Sweet Red Beans (p'at) are small and round and used widely in Korean confections. When cooked and mashed they are sweet and soft-textured. This sweet bean puree is used as filling in rice cakes and also now in donuts and rolls.

Todok is a fibrous white root found in the mountain in the spring. It must be pounded with a mallet and washed with salty water to take away its puckery taste before seasoning and cooking. It is an appetite stimulant.

Watercress (minari) is an aromatic plant used frequently in Korean cooking, especially the stems. It is not exactly the same as watercress but almost. The delicate leaves may be added to soups and are good with fish.

Most, if not all, of these ingredients may be purchased in Oriental groceries.

INDEX

INDEX OF KOREAN RECIPE TITLES